Tangled Thoughts
"UNRAVELING THE COMPLEX THREADS OF THE TEENS MIND"

SAAMIA SHAHID

BLUEROSE PUBLISHERS
India | U.K.

Copyright © Saamia Shahid 2024

All rights reserved by author. No part of this publication may be reproduced, stored in a retrieval system or transmitted in any form or by any means, electronic, mechanical, photocopying, recording or otherwise, without the prior permission of the author. Although every precaution has been taken to verify the accuracy of the information contained herein, the publisher assume no responsibility for any errors or omissions. No liability is assumed for damages that may result from the use of information contained within.

BlueRose Publishers takes no responsibility for any damages, losses, or liabilities that may arise from the use or misuse of the information, products, or services provided in this publication.

For permissions requests or inquiries regarding this publication, please contact:

BLUEROSE PUBLISHERS
www.BlueRoseONE.com
info@bluerosepublishers.com
+91 8882 898 898
+4407342408967

ISBN: 978-93-6452-010-2

Cover design: Daksh
Illustrations: Rashid Shahid
Typesetting: Tanya Raj Upadhyay

First Edition: December 2024

Dedicated to my late grandfather, Masood Ahmed, my Nana Baba. Your love and encouragement will always be cherished.

To my amazing mother, father and brother for their unwavering support and love. You three are the most important and special people in my life. I love you so much, more than words can express

Sincerely,

Saamia,

Tangled Thoughts

Dear Reader,

Welcome to Tangled Thoughts. If you've ever felt like your mind is a maze of questions, dreams, and emotions, you're not alone. I started writing poetry when I was eight, trying to capture all the things I felt but couldn't always say. Like many of us, I've faced moments of self-doubt, of wanting to be understood, of searching for my place in the world—and I've found that putting words to those feelings helps make them a little clearer.

The poems in this book are pieces of my journey so far, through the ups and downs of being a teenager. Maybe, like me, you've wondered who you are or where you're going. Maybe you've felt the need to fit in, or the desire to stand out, or simply the urge to understand yourself. I think we all feel that way sometimes, and that's what connects us.

I hope that as you read, you find lines that speak to you, moments that remind you of your own path, and words that make you feel seen and understood. Growing up can feel overwhelming, but we're all figuring it out together, one thought, one feeling, one poem at a time. Here's to the shared experience of being young, and to finding our way forward, side by side.

With love,
Saamia Shahid

Table of Contents

Words 2
Positive 5
Party 6
Chicken Soup 8
My Parents 9
Diversity 10
Beautiful Nature 13
I Love India 16
Sandy Shores 21
Would You Like to Go? 23
Love 26
Nana Baba 28
Dadi and Dada 30
Nanu 32
Weather 34
Home 37
Qatar 39
My Wonderland 43
Questions 47
Is it Wrong? 50
Am I A Poet? 55
My Boat Life 56
Boredom 57
Lost 59
Stranded 61

Listlessness	63
Uncertain and Insecure	64
Ocean	66
Fire	68
Chained to A Path	70
Illusion	72
The Silent Aftermath	75
Muddled Up	76
Who am I really?	78
Terrible Strife	80
Stresses	82
Dreaded Disease	86
2021	88
Perfection	93
Prepared	96
Undying Nervousness	99
Competition	101
Test Anxiety	103
C+	105
I'm Ready	106
Determination	108
Raging Anger	110
Emotional Change	112
Fallen Planet	114
No One Understands	117
Who am I?	119
Writer's Block	121

Sleepy	123
Locked Heart	124
Hidden Thorns	126
My Egocentric Envy	129
Loss	132
Acceptance	134
My Father	138
Introduction to the author:	140

It all falls down, they say
Living a full life, but only halfway
If I've learned one thing, it'd be this
That dreaming's only dreaming
If you're not afraid to miss
Sleep Walking, Cinders

Words

Words are so powerful,
They can make someone's day,
They can make all your problems drift away,
They can make you cry,
Or they can just be big, fat lies.

Words are so powerful,
They can be sour, sickly and scary,
Rude, cruel and contrary,
Mean and vicious,
Or maybe honest and conspicuous.

Words are powerful,
They can be artificial,
Lies and unofficial,
Or sweet, but so untrue,
A cunning lie too.

Words are so powerful,
Words can be expressive,
Intellectual and impressive,

Words can change a soul,
They can take you on quite a stroll.

Words are so powerful,
They can be like honey,
I think these words have more value than money,
Dripping with care and kindness,
Showcasing great politeness.

Words are so powerful,
They can be strong, kind and true,
This is the kind of vocabulary I would like to pursue,
Words have great meaning,
With the right ones, you could succeed.

Words are so powerful,
Be careful which ones you choose,
They can be ruthless and hurtful, all kinds of abuse,
A kick in the gut,
A slap on the face,
All kinds of disgrace.

Words are so powerful,
So, listen, oh I pray,
Let us think about the words we say,
Is it compassionate? Is it sincere?
In the end of the day,
Being considerate deserves a cheer!

Positive

When life gives you troubles,
Skip a-long on the street,
Don't see problems, see the opportunities,
A way to prove yourself and show personality.

Smell the flowers,
Not the fertilizer,
The sun is up,
Now your day is all brighter!

You let go of grudges,
Now you're a lot lighter,
When life croaks at you,
Sing along,
Just chill out,
You can be strong!

Skipping about a meadow,
Discovering a newfound bliss,
Life is a great adventure,
Full of mystery and twists.

Calm down,
Don't get too upset,
You'll feel better I bet!

Party

I'm feeling a little vibe,
I need to party,
Forget all my problems,
I need to party.
Let it all go,
Grasp the moment,
True colors show,
I'm feeling it in my bones,
Bring out the confetti,
I'm ready, are you?
Bring in the hugs,
Turn the music up!
I don't deny my love,
I don't avoid my problems,
But now, I'll party on,
Day and night, I've worked hard enough,
I know what I do,
I just chill,
Start anew,
Nobody to stop me,
Nobody to hurt me,
Everybody loves me!
I feel like I'm free!
I need to party!

Chicken Soup

Creamy, warm and delicious,
Clears up my throat,
Chewy chicken and warm liquid,
It feels good in my tummy,
As I sip, I know it's super yummy,
It's called chicken soup,
I'd like it any time,
To hate it is such a crime,
The warmth I feel in my throat,
It calms me down,
It tastes so nice,
A lovely delight,

My Parents

You take care of me when I'm sick,
With something I need, you're quick.
There are times I make mistakes,
But your patience never breaks.

You take me out to places,
In trouble, you'll hear my plea.
For all you've done and all you do,
I only wish I could repay you.

I love you both so dearly,
And hope to care for you one day too.
Keep you close, my love won't wane,
Dear parents, I love you.

Diversity

Dazzling colors, dark and bright,
Diverse, yet we still divide and fight.
Battles lost, hearts torn,
Dreams left tattered and worn.

Discrimination circles the earth,
Mocking our differences, denying worth.
Black, blue, green, and pink—
It's your thoughts that make us blink.

Indian, Arab, Spanish, too,
Portuguese, American—histories true.
We've stumbled, faltered, and it shows,
But now's the time to let love grow.

To see each soul, beyond the skin,
To let compassion be where we begin.
Differences can be a light, not a wall,
A bridge to lift, not a means to fall.

Let's embrace this truth, no longer ignore
I have my ways, and you have yours.
Together we stand, different but strong,
In harmony's song, where we all belong.

Beautiful Nature

There's a beautiful place,
Uncluttered space, a world of scenes—
No litter, no trash,
Fresh scents in the breeze,
Clear waterfalls, copious streams.

We are jubilant,
Branches sway in the wind—
This joy is forevermore.

The sunrise casts its joyful glow,
Dawn painted in orange and blue.
I lay on the mossy floor,
Feeling loss no more.

My eyes grow heavy,
I am one with the land.
The moss is my bed,
The sky is my ceiling,
This is my place—
I close my eyes.

Hand dipped in a cool, crystal lake,
Morning dew beneath my feet.
The all-encompassing fog rolls in,
Wrapping me whole, calm within.

The morning mist,
Delicate blooms,
Trees as tall as towers loom.

Moss cradles all in a gentle embrace,
The chill wind cools my cheeks,
Oh, serendipitous land,
My heart you now keep.
I surrender to the quiet sound,
And dream until the world awakes.

I Love India

I am from India,
An intriguing place,
Bustling streets,
The drama, the craziness.

Tears fall from the sky every monsoon,
Where my relatives are,
The enchanting smell of petrichor,
Historical sites, the mighty forests,
That amaze every tourist.

But I don't know you very well, India,
But I hope to, soon.
I want to learn my language,
To know the customs,
To relish the native foods,
To gaze at the trees.

India is a place,
Where I can be me.

I visit my distant family there,
I have some fun,
I see all sorts of animals on the streets!
Bulls, goats, and horses,
Cats, dogs, and more.

Everything gets hyped
When it starts to pour.
It's littered, yes,
Maybe even dangerous, yes,
But I will reunite anyways,
Yes, I will.

I love my country so,
I love it more than any other.
We went to Agra,
Had creamy malai,
Sweet lassi, and pani puri.

One day, I'll visit again,
In summer vacation.
For now, I'll wait and go through the school year,
Until I can be in mirth and cheer,
When I get to see India, my jewel,
Where my summers will always be cool!

Sandy Shores

Sandy Shores

The cool breeze,
The soft and ticklish sand,
The inviting, cool, great, body of water,
The rocks, the seaweed.

I step into the sea,
A wave hits and washes over me,
It feels so welcoming.

The sea sings pleasant tunes,
The mud and water greet me,
I am lost in its authenticity,
I depart when its dark,
I am soaking in serenity.

I feel so free,
Maybe we'll go dune buggying,
Rushing past the mountains of sand,
The feeling of the desert is simply grand,
This is a special land.

Would You Like to Go?

Get away from that screen,
Get away from that phone,
We're too addicted—
Close your eyes and break free!

Try something new,
Play a game or two,
Under the glorious sky,
Let's be who we are,
Jump to the stars,
And travel galaxies far.

Let's sing out loud,
Feel joy unbound.
I just want to get out,
I just want to be free.

Break the chains of addiction,
Relax our eyes,
Throw away the troubles,
Let them float to the skies.

Let's be kind,
Let's be nice,
Take my hand—
End this digital strife.
Let's stand together,
Now and forever.

Let's have fun all year,
Forget our fears.
We must enjoy,
Why not play with toys?
Rejoice in the snow,

Dance in the rain,
Breathe in blossoms sweet and fair,
Their fragrance floating through the air.

Let's calm our restless hearts,
Turn off the screens,
Let's make our own stories,
And live out our dreams.
No electronics today,
What do you want to play?
A game of tag?
Hide and seek?

Let's be together,
On the grass we'll run.
Come play with me, until the day is done—
Under the setting sun, let's chase the fun.

Love

A cuddly blanket,
Wrapped around,
A warm embrace,
Feeling appreciated.

Joyful as can be,
Whenever I'm in trouble,
You're there on the double.

Love comes in many forms—
Like my mom who gave birth to me,
My father, brother, and my relatives,
Even the dazzling couples on TV.

Regardless,
Love is as beautiful as can be.

Nana Baba

Full of life and surprise,
Yet incredibly intelligent and wise,
Always willing and fulfilling,
So amazing he would mesmerize.

Healthy and fit,
Committed to the bit,
Always ready for fun,
Never quit until he was done.

Sacrificed his pleasures,
His love beyond measure,
Playing games like table tennis,
His talent and energy so momentous.

But deep down he was a dreamer,
Always was a believer,
Saw past any flaws,
Refused to accept a lost cause.

He inspires me to be better,
To commit to the letter,
He wasn't perfect,
But he deserved all the respect.
Love you Nana Baba

Dedicated to my grandfather, Masood Ahmed

Dadi and Dada

I listen to their stories of old,
Of times when they were bold.
Their laughter echoes in the air,
Their wisdom and kindness, beyond compare.

We share simple moments, a smile, a meal,
It's in these times that I truly feel.
Dadi's gentle touch, her hand on my head,
Dada's hearty laugh, the words he said.

Their love crosses all distances and space,
It wraps me in a warm embrace.
I might not see them every day,
But their love is never far away.

They give me blessings, so sincere,
Even if we're apart most of the year.
Their voices calm, their faces bright,
They fill my heart with a glowing light.

Itna samajh bhi nahi a sakta hai,
Lekin koshish karletihu,
And I know they do it too.

No matter how far I roam,
With them, I always feel at home.

*Dedicated to my grandparents,
Shaik Fareed and Rasheeda Sultana*

Nanu

So sweet,
She would help me in a heartbeat,
So sweet,
She is always there for me,

Always prepared,
No one can compare,
Kind and fair,
Yet paranoid and aware.

She pushes me for more,
She knows I can soar,
Walking with her as the sun rises,
Hearing her wisdom even while I tire.

But I am a fiery soul,
Impulsive and emotionally driven,
Lava spouts out of my mouth,
And the next thing I know.

I wake up and I find that,
I messed up,
I know I've been terrible,
I'm simply unbearable.

But she comes like a wave,
She invites me with food I crave,
Welcoming me despite my outbursts,
Seeing the flower and looking past the dirt,

She comes right back after all the hurt,
A worried warrior that never stops,
She puts halt to my teardrops,
I love my Nanu, she is such a dear.

She cares about everyone,
Works so hard,
Her copious flow of patience,
And ubiquitous understanding,
Is simply everlasting,
I love you Nanu.

(Dedicated to my grandmother, Kausar Unissa)

Weather

The sunny days make you sweat,
The rainy days make you wet,
The misty days make it hard to see,
But positive, let's be.
There is no such thing as bad weather,
All of it can be lovely,
To truly enjoy,
On the sunny days, we spend outside,
We play and dance,
The sweltering heat,
The persistent sunbeams,
As I wipe my brow,
At the end of the day,
We are baked in the heat,
Never to forget all that fun,
Rainy days are my specialty,
I open my mouth for a taste of the sky's delicacy,
It tastes plain, but nonetheless,
I enjoy the wetness above the rest,
I open my arms and say,
"The rain is here, hooray!"
Rain, I love so much,

"You may get a cold, they say,"
Forget all that, later I will pay,
I spin around in circles,
In the end, I am soaking wet,
But afterward, I never feel regret,
There's the windy times,
The air rushes past my face,
But I think of it as an exuberant embrace,
The cool air feels so great,
As I let it go past my hair and my face,
Clothes are flowing, flags are flapping,
Any stubborn feelings are swept away,
Then there's snow,
Little snowflakes dance in the sky,
And reach the ground, making no sound,
You can make snow angels and snowmen,
You can make snowballs,
The white snow is like a blank canvas,
Up for interpretation and creation,
The weather is enticing,
The weather is beautiful.

Home

It's where the crickets chirp at night,
Where the rain pours hard,
I hear the soft thud of rain,
The incessant horns drive me insane.
Our balcony, which is poorly maintained,
With dirt and faded drawings remain,
The lovely smell of petrichor fills the air,
The neighbor's plants are kept with care.
The damp floors and wet stains,
Like a safety hazard, but I don't care.
The lush and evergreen forest outside,
Makes me feel so alive.
Small apartment on the inside,
Inside my heart for all time.
The soft putter of the fan,
As it spins without a plan,
Late nights with my cousin clan.
We played all night and ran and ran,
"In the distance, you can see Golconda Fort,"
My father would excitedly report,
Jumping in puddles on the court,
Mirthful feelings of all sorts,
Every summer, when I come,
I feel as bright as the sun!

Qatar

Qatar is where I live,
A land of peace, safe and sound,
It's the place I call home,
Where my roots are firmly found.

A mosaic of many nationalities,
Bringing life, color, and joy to our community.
So many chances to play, to laugh, to run,
Under the warm embrace of the Arabian sun.

Qatar's coastline stretches with beautiful beaches,
Golden sands as far as the eye reaches.
Summer sun shining bold and bright,
While December winds bring a gentle delight.

I've been in Qatar as long as I can recall,
Embraced by its warmth, its culture, its call.

The National Museum stands, a treasure to behold,
Preserving traditions, stories of old.
A desert rose, proud and grand,
Inviting tourists from every land.

Mosques serene, with domes that shine,
A call to prayer that feels divine.

The Souqs are lively, filled with cheer,
Fragrant spices, colorful goods appear.
A bustling market where stories unfold,
Every corner whispers tales untold.

From the modern skyline reaching high,
To the calmness of the desert, under a starry sky.
Qatar is diverse, grand, and sandy,
From the dunes to the palms, ever so handy.

A place where culture and progress intertwine,
Traditions thrive as the city shine.
Oh, how we adore the summer breeze,
When it whispers through the palms, swaying with ease.
-Whether it's a ride on a dhow in the sparkling bay,
Or an adventure in the dunes, where children play.

From vibrant festivals to peaceful nights,
Qatar is a land of countless delights.
It's more than just a place to live—
It's home, with endless stories to give.

My Wonderland

I am riding on my cloud,
Riding through the skies,
But I don't need it though,
I can fly,
I feel the wind in my hair,
I have no care,
Hop on, hop on,
You asked me where?
I don't know, anywhere,
I stand on my cloud,
Tall, happy, and proud,
I raise my hands up,
Something is coming out of me,
All my problems were gone in the air,
I am in my secret lair,
My cloud is comfy, inviting, and soft,
There are rainbows in the sky,
All the vibrant colors show,
Red, orange, yellow, green, blue and violet,
Gold and silver hues, too,
I close my eyes and grasp this moment tightly,
But it is,
Slipping away,

Reality is coming through,
My thoughts are lost,
I am back in the chains,
Back to all those studies,
Back to all those classes,
Oh, wonderland, when can I visit again?
I miss you,
I try to run from real life,
Reality is rapidly catching up,
I look back and face,
The bad memories of the past,
My dilemmas in the present,
And my worries for the future,
They haunt me,
My rainbow fades,
My cloud disappeared,
When can I go back,
To my Wonderland of cheer?

Questions

Why am I so stressed?
Why do I feel so blue?
Why should I just stand there?
Why am I so glum?
Why should I play along?
Why should I stand alone?
Who am I to talk?
Can I be amazing?
Will I succeed?
When can I just fly away,
And hop on my unicorn stead?
When can I just fly away?
And just be me?
When should I climb aboard,

My ship, *Pink Parade*?
Should I go or should I stay?
Why is this world so confusing?
Why does every mind have questions?
"Will coronavirus end?"
"When should I send my-
History project?"
Or when will I have real friends?
Who are we to ask?
Who am I to complain?
Where shall I aim?

Is it Wrong?

Is it wrong to be sensitive?
To be easily ripped apart in shreds?
Is it wrong to feel jealous?
To feel uneasy about someone's specialties?

Is it wrong to desire pleasure?
When I should focus on tasks instead?
Is it wrong to despise?
Simply being alive?

Is it wrong to feel angry?
In a blessed and privileged life?
Is it wrong to feel tired?
Useless and uninspired?

Is it wrong to want to hurt?
To crush something into pieces?
Is it wrong to feel crazy?
Misunderstood and hazy?

Is it wrong to feel like a waste of space?
Thinking of yourself as a useless disgrace?
Is it wrong to want more?
To break free and explore?

Is it wrong to be confused?
Have no idea what is happening?
Is it wrong to make mistakes?
To desire moving backwards like a wave?

Is it wrong to be yourself?
To be wild and crazy and yell?
Is it wrong to say you're a human?
When deep inside you know you're like a demon?

Is it wrong?

Am I A Poet?

I try so hard,
Every idea is written,
Or sometimes discarded.

I like poetry—
It's the sound of leaves in the breeze,
It's the chirping of birds at dawn,
It's love drifting like petals in spring,
But no matter what, my tongue stays drawn.

Still, I try so hard,
Yet, am I a poet?
Are my words any good?
If only I could share my lines,
But I'm too shy,
I wonder, "Would they like it? Would they care?"
I don't know, and it's hard to bear.

My dad says so, he thinks it's true,
But deep inside, I still don't know.
Would it be good?
Will I fail?
I may not know if I'm a poet,
But I'll keep writing, even if unsure.

My Boat Life

I feel like I'll sink,
Maybe I'll float?
Who knows? I am on a boat.

Life is a sea,
We can simply sail,
Unpredictable and unsafe,
But enough thinking,
We must hurry,
Or we'll be late.

Boredom

Boredom breathes its painful curse upon me,
I feel like I am useless,
I feel so bored,
Time goes incredibly slow,
Nothing is done,
Boredom plagues us all,
Nothing to do,

Lost

Lost in my rowboat,
I don't see a thing,
My lamp is out already,
So far, my boat is steady.

I hear many voices,
Some giving directions, some giving curses,
Each instruction is different,
Can't tell my left from right,
I hug myself, overwhelmed in fright.

Questions bombard my mind; will I live through the night?
Why am I here? You may ask,
I am on a very interesting task,
But I'm lost, alone and I don't know where to go,
I have hopes and dreams,
I refuse to look back,
Uncertainty is certain, that's all I know,
As I sit here, in the dark, stranded,
Alone.

Stranded

I'm stranded on an island,
I'm lost and I'm alone,
I'm stranded on an island,
And I haven't got my phone.

Sweat trickles down my forehead,
And I feel so awake,
I know that it's my time,
When I feel the earth shake,
No one can help me,
But I am just fine,
My island is a continuous storm,
And it is all mine.

Sunshine and storms come around as well,
Being on this island isn't always so swell,
My island keeps fluctuating,
It can be a little frustrating,

But my island is mine,
And I'll look on wistfully,
By the coastline,
Maybe one day I'll have the courage to explore,
Until then, I'll stay by the shore,

Listlessness

My feet feel like jelly,
Just wait, I'm not ready,
I don't know what to do.

My head is a rock,
The clock goes tick-tock,
My arms are heavy noodles.

I am strangely tranquil—but not like a Buddha,
My legs are hefty blocks.
I feel like tugging out my hair;
Sometimes, life is just not fair.

I want to just go back to bed,
Listen to music, take a nap instead.

Uncertain and Insecure

Bubbling pot inside,
Many thoughts lie,
What does my future hold?
Why is it hard to be bold?
Am I doing things right?
Am I holding on too tight?
Should I simply let loose?
And try to go with the flow?
Many outcomes to show?
I'm not even comfortable in my own skin,
Do I really need to go for the win?
I try and aim to be the best,
My skills and determination put to the test,
Uncertain future,
Worries me,
What is my destiny,
Do I want to be free?
What would I do if I was?
Some die, some are born,
Every second, my spirit feels torn,
Who am I?
I helplessly cry,
I am insecure,
I can be crazy,
I enjoy politeness,

But can be pretty lazy,
Every page in my life has details,
I stumble, crumble, and many times, I fail,
I let out a sigh and a wail,
I'm busy, but can I find time to spare?
Don't know what to do,
My head is a maze,
When will I get out of this phase?
Perhaps one of these days,
I can be like a fiery volcano,
I can also be a firmly rooted tree,
I've got all these versions and moods,
But in the end, I'm just me,
I am just me.

Ocean

I have a friend,
Her name is Ocean,
She puts me in a trance,
When she does her tide dance.

It's like a potion,
She's so lovely,
In motion.

Her rushing waves,
The sounds she makes,
That makes her,
A saving grace,
Blue reflecting water,
Feelings of freedom,
The wonder, under, never dies,
She fills me with peace,
Soaks up my tears,
Puts rest to my fears,
Like almost nothing can go wrong,

A mystifying sensation,
God's gifts,
A true, incredible and astounding miracle,
Letting my dear friend Ocean, Carry me,
As I close my eyes,
And drift away like the tides.

Fire

Merry, crackling fire,
Go a little higher,
Keep giving me merry warmth,
Keep enticing me with your gaze,
Dazzling campfire.

Always keeps me amazed,
But I don't take any chances,
I don't come too close.

I know my limits,
Fire can cause strife,
Also, like tyrannical destruction,
Hurts as much as it heals,
Burns and seals,
Fire is life.

Chained to A Path

I am chained to a path,
That others chose,
Nothing is free, not even my toes.
I thought I was free,
I am nowhere close,
I cannot lose.

I don't know,
What I want,
I just want to make my parents proud,
I'm airy and mindless like the clouds,
Fluid and shapeless like the water,
Yet fiery and furious like the fire.

As well as rough and rigid like the earth,
But I don't know what I want
Or how to go through life,
Laziness encompasses my lack of certainty,
In this sense, I don't mind being chained down,
My life is not necessarily mine to live,
I need to respect what my parents give,
So, until the end, I will go with their flow,
Will I be happy? Successful?
Who really knows?

Illusion

Illusion, I can't see anything right,
Illusion, is this all a fantasy?
Illusion, what is wrong or right?
Illusions keep me awake at night,
Illusions of the past,
Illusions of a better future,
Illusions like a blast,
Illusions like my sutures,
Illusions of dawn and dusk,
Illusions of the flame and rust,
Illusions that I always see,
What is happening to me?
Illusions are a fickle thing,
The lovely songs that it sings,
I see, and hear lovely birds,
But it's an illusion, it was the telephone,
I breathe illusions,
I can feel illusions,
Is this a dream?
What do I see?
What am I meant to believe?
The cup of illusions stirs by the day,
I don't want to be asleep,
I don't want to be awake,
I hate the loud,
I despise the quiet,
But what if it is all illusions,
And the silence is loud?

The Silent Aftermath

A silent environment after a celebratory event,
Little remains, everyone content,
Alone is I, ceasing to clean,
After all I have seen.

The guests were talkative and charming,
The silence is subtle and calming,
The mess in the aftermath, alarming.

A quite clean up takes place,
Afterwards it is a spotless, deserted place,
Excitement dying down, streamers hiding in sight.
Fulfilling cake,
Singing silence,
Housemaids keep sweeping,
Vacuum sounds, all around,
The silent aftermath.

Muddled Up

So much I want to write on paper,
Words are never enough,
I take a deep breath, inside out.

Why can living be so tough?
I don't understand why,
I don't understand how,
I used to be so wild and carefree,
No cares in the world, I would sing.

But I never knew,
Hardship grew,
So very confused.

Don't have the courage,
To break the rules,
Timid and afraid,
I worry too much,
Thinking about the past,
But it stays the same.
The present is my decision,
But I don't have precision,
I share that I am, confident,
But I'm powerless,
Intelligent, But I lack intellect,

Who am I really?

Who am I?
I appear to others,
Positive and bright.
But I don't think that's me,
I just don't see,
What is so good about me?
What am I special for?
Do I have a part in the world?
I don't understand anything.

It's all a daze,
I'm so confused,
It's hard not to blow a fuse,
Emotions are complicated,
Why do I feel so overrated?
My paths are filled with mist,
As I try to figure out,
Why am I like this?
Who am I?

I am so messed up,
I just don't understand,
I'm so confused,
Everything goes against the plan,
Why do I think so much?
There is so much wrong with me,
Until then, I'll try to find my peace,
Only then, I'll feel truly free.

Terrible Strife

My mind is cluttered,
My heart is hurting,
Work is important,
Grades are a huge worry,
A shame we all live of this,
Horrible strife,
It's a thing,
Called life.

Stresses

My skills don't work,
My pen is idle,
My brain is cluttered,
My heart aches so, I feel pressured.

I always go with the flow,
But something just bothers me,
I wish to live and feel free,
Chains will come,
My wonderland will leave,
I repeat ideas,
I feel stupid.

Will I ever get through it?
I long to be,
Happy and free,
My thoughts safe,
No one will see,
No one can touch,
I wish this such,
I want to give happiness,
I want ease,
I wish to feel,
I wish to believe,
I hate to lose,
I love to win,
I worry about my fate,
And my fluid soul,

What if I change?
To something worse?

To always follow the flock,
That is a curse.
I am so distracted,
I need to keep my mind straight,
One of the top priorities is education,
My mind is blank,
Every day feels like walking on the plank,
It's all so confusing.

Will someone help me please,
I'm not kind,
I act recklessly,
Sometimes I wish I was blind,
To all these horrible things,
I'll survive, right?
I don't want to fail,
Life is like a market,
And my shop is crashing,
Plummeting to the ground,
Please don't blame me for being off topic,
I am simply expressing myself,
I think I will merely blurt all my troubles,
Thoughts, issues, and concerns,
Someday I want all these troubles to get out of my way.

Dreaded Disease

This dreaded disease,
The unwanted pest,
Does as it pleases,
Never rests.

A scary beast, you're having a feast,
I just wish you would just go,
You are the Corona-virus,
Infecting and plaguing people.

You've taken so many,
Yet you want more,
You tried my family,
And my relatives,
They fought and were set free.

Yet you still stick around,
Like heavy snow,
My vacations were messed up,
And that is one of the reasons,
I truly hate you!

You plagued schools and caused drama,
You caused lots of trauma,
Now I can't go to places,
You have arrested us all!

Why can't you just leave?
You keep breeding,
On us you are feeding,
It's because of you I can't even go to the masjid to pray,
One of the many reasons why I despise you,
Every day!

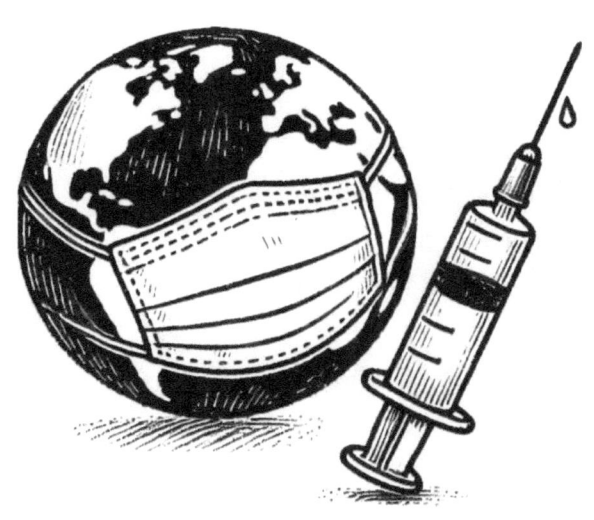

2021

2021, Is no fun,
I really thought,
"Something was to be done,"

But I'm stuck at home,
Most are on their phones,
I don't go out,
Unless it's grandma's house.

That's one of my only places of enjoyment,
At this point in time,
I've run out of words that rhyme,
No mask? Pay a fine,

Everyone in doubt,
Some that silently push,
"I have nothing to do all day,"
"I've finished all my work,"
"I've even created many paintings,"

"I've cleaned up the whole house!"
"My cousins have gone crazy!"
"He's talking to a mouse?"

I've just lost hope this year,
Summer vacation? But there's no cheer,
I want to go to malls,
Tired of pacing in my home hall,
Why don't vaccines have any effect?

What is going on?
The news is so depressing,
So sad to look upon.

Let me try binge-watching?
How about prime?
Finished all the shows there in no time,
How about Netflix?
Done already in a click.

Rewatching episodes and endless screentime,
All to distract from the reality, to feel in line,
Like we have control over something, anything,
Those times were really one of the worst,
So bad some ended up in a hearse.

So terrifying that it felt like a curse,
Day after day, night after night,
Ever since then, nothing ever really felt right.

Perfection

You must be the best,
Nothing short of new,
Perfect, above the rest,
Brimming expectations,
Brimming in a pot,
If you don't keep up with the flock,
You'll be left to rot,

Being yourself? It's just a lie,
But don't worry, it's okay,
It's quite normal now,
We just lie in our own way,
Judges aren't just in court,
They're all out there, everywhere,
You and I included,
And I know I'm not the only one,
Who feels like it's all unfair,

Fake your way into glory,
Fake it all the way,
Just remember to change up the story,
It'll go a long way,

Wear your best dress,
Wear your highest heels,
Put on all the make-up you can,

Maybe you'll look half as good,
And just keep it fake the whole time,
Nobody likes what's true,

Lose weight and get thin,
Diet and always win,
Keep your mouth shut,
Everyone knows your every move,
And they think you're a loser,

Ignorance is bliss,
But it's hard to accomplish this,
Oh, just 'don't care about what they think,'
But that's no piece of cake,
Growing up, you'll hate it all in your heart,
Trust me, it's true,

I question myself; "Don't I have a voice?"
Then why does it feel like I don't have a choice?

Prepared

Cough from dust,
Fire and ashes have scarred me enough,
Each breath tastes of smoke,
And I cringe at the wounds,
Every ache a reminder,
Overwhelming pain,
A pulse of madness,
Echoing in my mind.

I thought I was ready,
I trained for the worst this world could throw,
Hardened my heart,
Steeled my soul,
But now, as the storm rises,
I wonder—am I truly prepared?

Will I stand or will I fall?
There's only one way to know,
Let's see, let fate reveal,
What I'm truly made of.

Undying Nervousness

I feel my face go red and hot,
Like a steaming pot.
I gather courage,
But walk like a sloth.

People watch me;
I clench my fists,
Clear my throat,
Open my mouth—
A series of mumbles escape out.

I look north, I look south,
Wait... what were we talking about?
No one listens to me, so I don't listen to them.
Feeling ignored,
Right now, I just want to be alone.

Surrounded, everything is fuzzy,
The nervousness of the awkward—I sigh,
This problem may never die.

Competition

Didn't come to lose,
Neither did you,
I'm a grenade,
My personality steals the day,
Get out of the way.

You're here for shame,
Maybe that's why I came,
You are crushed and mushed,
Stuffed with fake confidence,
I'll be the winner,
You'll simply end up as dinner.
Get out of my way,
You're here for shame,
And that's why I came.

Test Anxiety

Will I ace the test?
I hope I do- I only wish for the best,
But it's taking a while,
Will my score make me smile?

I don't know if I've practiced enough,
It seems quite tough,
I hope at some point it gets easy,
The thought of tests make me queasy,

I'm sure I do have the smarts,
As I try to ace all the parts,
I need a seven or eight, just that please,
I studied, I hope it will be a breeze,

I care deeply for my grades,
As long as I score great, I'm ready for praise,
I don't want a four or a five,
I need more than that, I have a will to thrive,

I wish to get good grades all the time,
If I don't it is such a crime,
I need to ace all my tests in the future,
If I don't, then I'll be nothing but a loser,

C+

I got a C+ in History,
How? That's a mystery,
It's hurting my heart,
It's haunting me crazily,
Controlling my thoughts,
It's bombarding me bizarrely,
The news pierced me like a knife,
This is a terrible grade,
The worst in my life,
I want to scream and shout,
How could I receive something so horrible?
I'm dead without a doubt,
This grade is like a monster,
A surprise, silent, dark and scary,
I am so disappointed,
So will my parents be when they see,
They know that this grade isn't the best from me,
I feel ashamed,
Is this failure who I'm meant to be?

I'm Ready

I'm ready for the dragons,
I'm ready for the ride,
I'm ready to face the foes I know,
I'm going to survive,
With passion, I thrive,
Sparkles from the dust,
With your love, I'm alive,
Sparks to start a flame,
No more agonizing pain,
My blood flows copiously,
I break the bounds,
Worse than a hound,
Chains and smithereens,
I'm ready to face you, destiny.

Determination

My eyes burn,
My stomach churns,
But I keep going on,
I'm going to keep strong,

No matter how cold,
I will be bold,
I may lose breath,
But I don't fear death,

Go on and try to hurt me, fire,
I do not tire,
This journey may be hard,
My feet bleed from the glass shards,

Time goes slow,
I used to rarely know,
I used waste my time,
Simply waiting for the stars to align,

But now, I travel on,
I will not fall for your cons,
I never travel slow,
I don't travel for show,

I will walk more,
Acid pours,
Lightning strikes,
But regardless, I will climb the heights!

Raging Anger

The burning embers in my heart,
Blazing fire, feelings within,
I want to wreck a city down,
I will drive my enemies to the ground,
I will squeeze an apple to the core,
When I enter, the chandeliers will crash,
On a rampage, growling loud,
In my rage, no one makes a sound,
Stomping around,
Loud like thunder,
The ruins I create, a wild wonder,
Tears escaping while I scream;
"It's not as it seems,"
But I am a monster,
Gnashing my teeth,
Inciting terror,
I am in trouble,
I may seem like the evil devil,
But you don't understand,
My story is different,
Behind each devil is a crying soul,
None of this was planned,
I feel fury,
I am enraged!

Emotional Change

Am I really like this?
Rude and filthy,
Why do I act like this?
Mean and ugly,
How can I change?
I'm a huge disappointment.

Why do I feel like this?
So stressed and filled with complaints,
I would be so happy,
And I used to always believe I could find a way through,
But now I ask myself,
What happened to you?
I used to believe.
Every obstacle a challenge,
Work, an adventure,
Sorrows temporary,
Stress never to exist,
But now I ask myself,
Why am I like this?

Fallen Planet

I can't see the stars,
Only the moon,
To think we are worthy,
To think we are royal,
To think we are true,
To think we are loyal,
What a lie,
And what is your alibi?
We are slithering snakes,
Men of sin.
Greats of greed,
We don't listen to those in need,
We multiply day by day,
Looking at our Earth in dismay,
We are imbeciles,
We are fools,
We all simply desire to 'look cool'.
You cannot lie to yourselves,
About the beasts in us,
About useless goals, useless wants,
We can be rude and mean,
We don't deserve,
But we never care,
We feast on other's fails,
Don't lie to yourselves, we are all part of a coup,

All of us in the troupe.
Earthquakes, rocks and rumble,
Sea levels rise,
Because of ice glaciers, not a big surprise.
The world is dying by the hour,
But we only care about power,
The ending will be sour.
Understand,
The lies we create,
A bottomless pit,
Come dear child, come sit,
Let me tell you the story of the fallen planet,
About how Earth is dead,
The rich are now on the Moon and Mars instead.

No One Understands

No one understands,
No one bothers,
People just care about themselves,
Because that's all that matters,
Every day, I'm stuck in my own cage,
Not visible, but it's there,
Everybody walking with their friends,
I'm alone because I pretend like I don't care,

Everyday it's like this,
Overwhelmed, so many things to do,
Everyday it's like this,
I know it well, because it's true,

No one understands me,
No one gets it at all,
Not my family, not anybody,
Under waves of worry, how can I stand tall?

I'm just falling,
In a deep, dark hole,
I'm just falling,
Everything is out of control,

Who am I?

Where am I?
No one ever knows,
I just don't know,
"I'm alright," I'd pretend,
I have no best friend,
Everyone has their pair,
But I don't have mine,
I'm spending all my time alone,
Maybe mindless on my phone,
Everywhere I'm lonely,
Is this who I'm meant to be?

I love my family, and my family loves me,
But I'm not sure they'd understand,
I open to them,
But I feel strangely shut out again,
I don't always like socializing,
I don't know what I like,
I just feel like crying,
There're just too many things,
But of course, you wouldn't get it,
Nobody ever does,
It's not disrespects,
It's not like I want to be rude,
Forgive my attitude.

Writer's Block

I'm blocked,
I'm choked,
I have nowhere to go,
I'm at a new low,

I have no ideas,
I'm out of juice,
I don't know what to do,
I've no clue,

I'm waiting for a spark,
Anything at all,
But now I just fall,
I've got a headache,

I don't know what to write,
I can't think at all.

Sleepy

I feel sleepy,
My eyes resisting,
I feel tired,
My yawning continues,
It's been quite the day,
All the way,
I don't want to run,
Believe me, I'm done,
My limbs are aching,
My head is heavy,
My walk is swaying,
Not steady,
Slow blinking,
Head to the side,
My heart is thumping,
Gladly alive,
They all want to play,
"Are you crazy?" I say,
I refuse to get up,
I just want to sleep…

Locked Heart

Every day is the same,
I wake up at 6 am,
Every day is so plain,
As I hide in my den,

I'm tired of school,
I'm tired of work,
The same stupid rules,
The same stupid jerks,

I'm feeling angry,
But I act like I'm fine,
But really, I want to cry,
The food is tasteless every time I dine,

I don't get fazed,
I'm like a rock,
Adventures I used to crave,
Now my heart is a lock,

I couldn't write poems,
I was too tired,
Too worried about enjoyment,
Too worried about being desired,

I eat less,
Starve during the day,
I'm such a mess,
But who cares anyway?

My heart hurts,
Like I'm being compressed,
I'm going berserk,
Could I be suppressed?

I used to be so happy,
I used to be so joyful,
But as I feel more unhappy,
I've lost the ability to be mirthful.

Hidden Thorns

Feelings are complex things,
Hard to handle,
As they jumping and spring,
Unpredictability at its finest,

A rush of adrenaline first,
A cry of desperation next,
A sudden urge or thirst,
Feelings always persist,

Especially the 'negative' ones,
They are thorns,
Coming in with devilish horns,
Infiltrating and getting comfortable in your mind,

Gaining fuel day by day,
They never go away,
But suddenly they strike,
Hurtling forwards like a knife,

All of a sudden, you-
Stabbed someone undeserving,
And there goes,
You've got a thorn,

But it's not in your garden,
It's in theirs,
You continue the painful cycle,
Feelings are a fickle thing,

It keeps going,
Thorns and weeds grow,
You can chop them off,
You can set them on fire,

But they always come back,
Sometimes, even higher,
But you never know,
Because it's unpredictability at its finest,

But one thing is clear,
There are feelings deep inside,
Dark and ingrown,
In hiding, deep underneath the roses,
Feelings that should be feared,

Because feelings are a fickle thing.

My Egocentric Envy

You're so talented,
You're simply special,
I loved the way you sounded,
The way you sing and shine,

I wish that talent was mine,
I can't imagine,
I can't explain,
How it is myself I disdain,

I see you shimmer like a star,
Just by being who you are,
I just want to crumble down and cry,
Because I wish that talent was mine,

I want to feel happy for you,
I really do,
My envy should not be misconstrued,
It comes from a place of admiration,

The desire to impress a nation,
The need to be recognized,
The wish to have attention,
The desperation to be special.

In a world filled with talent,
Where everything runs rampant,
In a world where it is necessary to show off,
I would hate to be a knock-off,

Your talent is incredible,
If only I had a droplet,
If only I had a taste,
I'm sure my life would be great,
Admiration, respect and popularity,
Uniqueness, distinctiveness, and singularity,
Reveled, honored and adored,
Never to be ignored,

I envy your hard work and talent,
The way you sing is simply divine,
The way you socialize and intertwine,
The way you act is sublime,
I just wish all of that was mine.

Loss

I go to the same house,
Everyone is laughing and talking,
But deep down we all know,
Someone is missing.

It was months ago,
It was on a Saturday,
It happened all of a sudden,
Faster than pressing a button.

The next day,
We were at the funeral prayer,
Tears stream down my eyes,
And soaking the carpet.

Days of visitors expressing their sorrows,
Sporting black clothing,
And exchanging condolences,
But despite all of this.

I cannot believe,
My mind is in shambles,
My eyes are a vivid red,
I cannot bring myself to say it,
But he has reached his resting bed.

I was a brat,
I took everything for granted,
And now he is gone,
And sometimes I think it is my fault.

In memory of my grandfather, Masood Ahmed. Nana Baba, I miss you.

Acceptance

Your life doesn't have to be perfect,
It's okay to feel wrecked,
It's acceptable to have certain feelings,
Like anger and regret,

The beautiful thing about humanity,
Is that everyone has a range of personalities,
No one is always a lovely and sweet angel,
No one is always a horrifying and maniacal devil,

There is always room for improvement,
Nothing needs to have incredible alignment,
Defections are ubiquitous,
Everyone has their own significance,

Failure is part of living,
It's part of the steps to succeeding,
Good grades, bad grades, it doesn't matter,
Don't let something like that make you shatter,

Conflict and wars occur,
Not something that I concur,
But together we can reach a consensus,
And undergo a beautiful metamorphosis,

There will always be problems,
Whether you are a simpleton or a scholar,
But there will always be light,
And with help, we can face our problems with might,

Life is not always a terrible strife,
You don't need to cut the pain away with a knife,
Make it through, there is always someone who will believe in you,
Enough pretending, I'll let you see me, and let me see you,

Accept vulnerabilities, imperfections, and pain,
Give a listening ear and give up on vain,
Accept people for who they are,
There's no *necessity* to compete, we can *both* be stars.

My Father

I look in the mirror and I see,
A fierce warrior staring back at me.
A fighter, a rule enforcer,
Pushing harder as deadlines grow closer.

I glance again, and I see,
A caring soul, with infectious glee,
Keeping up morale with optimism bright,
Like sunlight shining through the darkest night.

I gaze deeper and start to find,
A dreamer, with limitless ideas in mind,
Bringing fresh thoughts to the table,
Keeping the team strong and stable.

I observe the reflection staring back,
An intelligent mind that stays on track.
A businessman, sharp, astute, and wise,
His victories endless, his success no surprise.

I look in the mirror and I know,
That like him, I fight through ice and snow.
Yet I dream, I create, I delight,
In every challenge, he helps me with might.

Introduction to the author:

Saamia Shahid is a 15-year-old poet with a voice far beyond her years. As a tenth grader living in Qatar, Saamia captures the raw emotions and internal battles of adolescence with striking clarity and depth. Her poetry delves into the complexities of teenage life, from the constant tug-of-war between independence and family expectations to the existential questions that define her thoughts.

Writing since the age of eight, Saamia uses poetry as her outlet to process the world around her. In her debut collection, she fearlessly explores the struggles of identity, the challenges of excelling at school, and the universal quest for belonging. Each poem reflects the heart of a teenager navigating the stormy seas of growing up, while seeking understanding, connection, and purpose.

When she's not writing, Saamia enjoys reading, playing videogames, and spending time with her family and friends. Her first poetry book, *Tangled Thoughts*, offers a window into the mind of a young artist on the cusp of self-discovery.

www.ingramcontent.com/pod-product-compliance
Lightning Source LLC
LaVergne TN
LVHW041605070526
838199LV00052B/2995